THE WRITER'S POINT OF VIEW

NATIONAL BOOK LEAGUE NINTH ANNUAL LECTURE

N.B.L. Annual Lectures

THE USE AND ABUSE OF READING
by Sir Norman Birkett

SOCIAL HISTORY AND LITERATURE
by R. H. Tawney

LEISURE IN A DEMOCRACY
by Viscount Samuel

SOME THOUGHTS ON UNIVERSITY EDUCATION
by Sir Richard Livingstone

PHILOSOPHY AND POLITICS
by Bertrand Russell

HISTORY AND THE READER
by G. M. Trevelyan

I WANT! I WANT!
by John Masefield

THE WRITER'S POINT OF VIEW

W. SOMERSET MAUGHAM

LONDON
PUBLISHED FOR THE
NATIONAL BOOK LEAGUE
BY THE CAMBRIDGE UNIVERSITY PRESS
1951

The Ninth Annual Lecture of the National Book League, delivered by W. SOMERSET MAUGHAM, at the Kingsway Hall, W.C.2 on Wednesday October 24 1951, the Right Honourable SIR NORMAN BIRKETT in the Chair.

CAMBRIDGE UNIVERSITY PRESS
LONDON: BENTLEY HOUSE, 200 EUSTON ROAD, N.W.1
NEW YORK: 32 EAST 57TH STREET, NEW YORK 22
CANADA: THE MACMILLAN COMPANY OF CANADA LIMITED

All rights reserved

THE WRITER'S POINT OF VIEW

I AM very much afraid that you have been brought here under false pretences. You have been invited to listen to a lecture, but that is much too grand a name to use to describe the desultory remarks I propose to make. I am going to talk to you about reading and writing, not that I hope to tell you anything about them that you don't know already, but because it is with those two subjects that I have been during my life chiefly concerned. But before I begin I must tell you that I have been writing for very nearly sixty years and in that long time I have said pretty well everything I had to say. That I am now apt to repeat myself was borne in upon me a few years ago somewhat ruthlessly by an undergraduate at one of the great Universities who wrote to tell me that if ever he had to read again that the style of Swift was like a placid French canal bordered by poplars while the style of Dryden was like an English river meandering through green fields and past wooded hills, he would be sick. Mr. Eliot had not then published *Four Quartets* or I should have replied briefly with a quotation from *East Coker*, which runs as follows: "You say I am repeating something I have said before. I shall say it again". That charming and arrogant line may well serve to assuage the misgivings of many of us authors. I less courageously am merely going to take it for granted that no one in this Kingsway Hall has ever read a word I have written.

If I have been asked to address you to-day, it is not because I am a philosopher, an historian, an educationalist, a politician or a lawyer, but because I am a writer of fiction, and it is as such that I propose to speak to you.

After I had accepted your Director's flattering invitation, he sent me copies of the Annual Lectures that have been given by the National Book League during the last four or five years. I read them all with great interest, but none with greater interest than that which was delivered by Dr. Trevelyan.[1] In it he pointed out with great cogency the cultural and educational advantage it is to us to read history, but somewhat to my surprise he did not mention the fact that besides the useful lessons we may all get from the study of this subject we may also get a lot of enjoyment. I don't know what value historians to-day attach to Gibbon's *Decline and Fall of the Roman Empire* and to Macaulay's *History of England*, but I venture to suggest to you that they are uncommonly good reading. If you are not prepared to read them for your soul's good you can certainly read them for pleasure. It is true that Dr. Trevelyan insists that history should be readable, for otherwise only experts will read it and the layman will not gain the valuable instruction he so badly needs. In short he advocates the jam so that the powder may be palatable. The point I want to make is that we can swallow the jam regardless of the powder disguised by it.

Dr. Trevelyan did not see fit to remind you that the Muse of History has some poor relations whom she regards with condescension, but nevertheless makes use of when it suits her purpose. I hope you will not think it an impertinence on my part if I seek to mitigate the austerity of his Lecture by calling your attention to them. These are the journals and memoirs which various worthies have left if not for our edification, at least for our entertainment. English literature is not so rich in works of this kind as the French, but it is far from barren. Of course there is Pepys. I am sure you have all read with delight the journal that Boswell kept during the first year he spent in London and you have probably read the diaries of

[1] *History and the Reader*, National Book League; Cambridge University Press 1945, 2s. 6d.

Fanny Burney with her lively references to Dr. Johnson and her grim account of life as Second Keeper of the Robes to Queen Charlotte. I will only mention one more, since it seems to be little known, Lord Hervey's *Memoirs of the Court of George the Second*, but of course there are a number of others, Farington, for instance, which are eminently readable.

If we cannot boast of any memoirs that approach in interest the *Memoires* of Saint-Simon, we can at least flatter ourselves that we have produced in this island in Boswell's *Life* of Dr. Johnson the greatest biography that has ever been written. It is needless for me to say anything in its praise, but though in no way comparable I should like to remind you of Haydon's *Autobiography*. He was a poor painter, but he wrote in this a book that makes admirable bedside reading.

Your distinguished and learned President in the Lecture he delivered to you last year told you that the main purpose of reading is to instruct. That seems to me a very hazardous statement. It is as though you urged a man to play golf for the good of his liver rather than for the fun of the game. I am going to tell you something very different. I am going to tell you that the main purpose of reading is to entertain. But I must add quickly that not only what amuses entertains, but also what interests. You will not find much to amuse you in *Anna Karenina* and in Stendhal's *Le Rouge et le Noir*, but they are as interesting as *The Pickwick Papers* and *Huckleberry Finn* are amusing; and so, as entertaining.

The object of the National Book League is to induce people to read. But you are not likely to do that unless you can persuade them that reading is a pleasure rather than a chore. Obviously there are books that people have to read for a definite purpose, because they want to pass examinations, because they want to acquire information to put to some special use, or because they want to satisfy their curiosity, but then they do not read for pleasure. Of course I am not so foolish as to deny that you may get a lot of pleasure while you are reading in order to acquire information or to satisfy your curiosity. Such books as those of Professor Eddington, such a work as Bertrand Russell's *History of Western Philosophy* are as entertaining as any novel and as easy to read. All I wish to impress upon you is the admirable virtue of reading purely for pleasure without any ulterior motive. To acquire the habit of reading is to form for yourself a defence against most of the ills of life; it will enable you to bear a cold in the head with patience and the pangs of unrequited love with fortitude. But it is a habit that should be acquired early and no one is likely to acquire it unless the books that come to his hand afford him pleasure. To tell a boy that he *ought* to read this, that or the other is to excite in him at once a disinclination to read it. Pastors and masters are very ill-advised to scold the young for reading trash. They read it because it interests them. You may wish that they would read books which happen to interest you more, but you cannot force anyone's interest and the important thing is that the youth whose taste you seek to guide should enjoy what he reads. You may think he is wasting his time, but is it ever waste of time to do something that gives you pleasure?

A learned professor in one of the American Universities published some years ago a work entitled *How to Read a Book*. I have read it and will tell you something about it in a moment. Another professor has written a work called *How to Read a Novel*. This I have not read and so can't tell you anything about it. For all I know a third professor has produced a book named *How to Read a Short Story* and I shouldn't be surprised to hear that still another is engaged on one on *How to Read the Comics*. This should be an important guide when you consider that the Comics are the chief, if not the only reading of large sections of the adult public both in Europe and America. The author of *How to Read a Book* gives his students a number of rules to follow. One is never to read a book in an armchair, but seated at a desk with a pad and a pencil beside them. Then he recommends them to gather together in the evening, armed with their copious notes, and under the leadership of one of their party discuss the book chosen for the occasion, and he suggests the points they should discuss. The professor gives in his book a portentous list of the works he advises his students to read and among them are three of Dickens's novels. I would give a lot to be privileged to attend the meeting at which these admirable young people deal exhaustively with the moral, economic and psychological problems presented by *The Pickwick Papers*. If in the work I am telling you about more than a fleeting reference occurs to the possibility that any enjoyment can be got out of reading the books, many of them certainly well worth reading, that the learned professor offers for the instruction of his students, it has escaped me. To my mind he has made what should be a pleasure into a hideous bore, and I should have thought effectively eradicated from those young minds any inclination ever to open a book again after they were freed from academic bondage. Now, I have little doubt that many of you who have been good enough to listen to me will object that to read merely for pleasure is nothing but what in recent years has come to be disparagingly known as escapism. It is. I don't know what bright critic conceived the idea expressed by that word, but it was seized upon by many people who should have known better and for some time to describe a book as escapist was roundly to condemn it. You still see the word used by the less intelligent reviewers to whom it has never occurred that all literature is escapist. In fact that is its charm. Do we read Shakespeare's Sonnets or Keats's Odes for anything but the delight they give us? Do we read the novels of dear Jane Austen for any other reason? We may agree with the poet who said that life was real and life was earnest, but it has its lighter moments and there is no reason why we should not take advantage of them. I know no better way of doing this than by reading a book that entertains us. Now, that misguided critics should take exception to a book because it does no more than entertain would be of no great consequence, since, if it pleases, readers will read it notwithstanding, were it not for its effect on the writer. It is significant that so learned and scrupulous a scholar as Dr. Trevelyan seems to have thought it necessary in his Lecture to assure you that to read history is not mere hedonistic escapism. I should like to persuade you that if it were it would be none the worse for that.

But it is on us novelists that the fear of being charged with escapism has had what I consider its most unhappy effect. It has infected us with an uncomfortable sense of guilt. With the world in confusion, with the future uncertain, with freedom menaced, we cannot but ask ourselves whether we are justified in devoting the best of our lives to such a frivolous pursuit as writing novels. And when we are told that it is our business, not merely to entertain, but to deal with the pressing problems of the day, social security, economic inequalities, racial questions and what not, we sit up and take notice. We are tempted. We are no more modest than the rest of the human race and it appeals to our vanity to think that we can instruct our fellow-men and improve their lot. It gives us a pleasant sense of responsibility and indeed puts us almost on a level of respectability with the Directors of the Bank of England. We are tempted and sometimes we fall. But unfortunately to use the novel as a platform or a pulpit is fraught with danger. If the novelist concerns himself with current affairs he runs the risk that when the affairs cease to be current his novel will cease to be readable. That it what has happened to the later novels of H. G. Wells and no one was better aware of it than Wells himself. The novelist runs the same risk when he concerns himself with the fashionable fads of the moment. I read an article recently in which the author asserted that in future no novel could be written except on Freudian principles. That seemed to me a very rash statement. Most psychologists, while acknowledging the value of Freud's contribution to their science, are of opinion that he put many of his theories in an exaggerated form; but it is just these exaggerations that attract the novelist because they are striking and picturesque. The psychology of the future will doubtless discard them and then the novelist who has based his work on them will be up a gum tree.

But please do not misunderstand me. There is no reason why the novelist should not deal with any subject under the sun and enrich it with all the ideas he is happy enough to be possessed of so long as he is prepared to accept the limitations of his medium. The novel is a form of art, perhaps not a very exalted one, but a form of art nevertheless, and the purpose of art is to please. If in many quarters this is not acknowledged I can only suppose it is because of the unfortunate impression so widely diffused that there is something shameful in pleasure. I presume that arises because when people think of pleasure they connect it with the pleasure of the senses, which is natural enough because they are the most vivid. But there are also the pleasures of the spirit and some of us, especially as we grow old, are so fortunate as to find a delight in them as great as in the pleasures of the senses. All pleasure is good. Only some pleasures have mischievous consequences and it is better to eschew them. Of course there are intelligent pleasures and unintelligent pleasures. I venture to put the reading of a good novel among the most intelligent pleasures that man can enjoy.

Let us consider for a moment what are the qualities a novel should have in order to afford the reader the intelligent pleasure he has the right to demand. It should have a coherent and probable story, a variety of plausible incidents, characters that are living and freshly observed and natural dialogue. It should be written in a style that is suited to the matter. If the novelist can do that he has done all that should be asked of him. His business is to please, not to instruct.

I must tell you, however, that not all novelists agree with me. Some time ago I was reading the page which one of the best of our weeklies devotes to the criticism of current literature. The reviewer started his consideration of a new novel with the words: "Mr. So and So is not a mere story-teller". The word *mere* stuck in my throat, and on that day, like Paolo and Francesca on another occasion, I read no further.

The reviewer in question is himself a well-known novelist, and though I have never been so fortunate as to read any of his works, I have no doubt that they are meritorious. I am told, indeed, that he has a large and faithful public who look forward to the appearance of his latest novel with the same sort of eagerness as fashionable women look forward to the latest creations of Christian Dior or Jacques Fath. From the words I have just quoted to you I can only surmise that he looks upon the telling of a story as a trifling matter and that in his opinion a novelist should be something more than a novelist. For my part I think it is enough if a novelist is a good novelist. The novelist should know a little about a great many things, but it is unnecessary for him to be a specialist on any particular subject. He need not eat a whole sheep to know what mutton tastes like, it is enough if he eats a chop. Applying then his imagination and his creative faculty to the chop he has eaten he can give you a very good idea of an Irish stew. But when he goes on to give you his views on sheep raising, the wool industry and the political situation in Australia, I think it is wise to accept them with reserve. Only the very ingenuous can suppose that the novel can teach us the things that it is most important for us to know.

The novelist is by his very nature biassed. There is no such animal as the mere story-teller. The novelist is at the mercy of his bias. The subjects he chooses, the characters he invents and his attitude towards them are conditioned by it. Whatever he writes is the expression of his personality and it is the manifestation of his innate instincts, his feelings, his experience and his opinions. However hard he tries to be objective he remains the slave of his idiosyncracies. However hard he tries to be impartial he cannot help taking sides. He loads his dice, sometimes not knowing what he is doing, but sometimes knowing very well, and then he uses such skill as he has to prevent the reader from finding him out. You will remember that Henry James insisted again and again that the novelist must dramatize. That is a telling, though not perhaps very lucid way of saying that he must arrange his facts in such a way as to capture and hold your attention. That means that if need be he will sacrifice verisimilitude and credibility to the effect he wants to get. That, as we know, is what Henry James constantly did, but of course it is not the way a work of scientific or informative value is written. The aim of the writer of fiction, I repeat, is not to instruct, but to please. If readers want to inform themselves on the pressing problems of the day they will do well to read, not novels, but the works that specifically deal with them.

Before ending this part of my discourse I should like to

mention a practice, adopted first, I think, in America, but now followed by some English publishers, which to my mind is of considerable service to readers. This is the practice of putting on the jacket of a book what amounts to a short biography of the author. This of course is well worth doing with works of information where it is important to know the qualifications of the person whose book you are invited to read. But it is worth while doing also with works of the imagination. You may say that you are only concerned with the book and what sort of person the author is, what sort of life he has led, has nothing to do with you. I am not sure you would be right. I was once commissioned by an American publisher to write prefaces to ten of the world's greatest novels and in order to do this to my satisfaction I found it necessary to acquire more than a superficial acquaintance with the lives of their authors. It added to my interest in the novels I was dealing with and increased my appreciation and my understanding of them. If, for instance, you have learnt from the jacket that the origins of a popular author were humble and his early life one of considerable hardship you can make allowances for the fact that he consistently represents characters in a higher class as scoundrels and nit-wits. You can regard with indulgence what otherwise would seem to you merely silly. To know something about your author may also affect the value you place on a book. Some years ago a short novel was published which was greatly admired by the intelligentsia. I was asked by a friend of mine what I thought of it. "That depends on how old the author is," I answered. "Why, what has that got to do with it?" he asked. "A great deal," I replied. "If it was written by a young man just down from the university I think it's interesting and clever. It has the obscurity, the complication, the parade of sophistication, the literary affectations which cultured youth naturally indulges in. That doesn't matter. There's enough promise in the book to suggest that as he grows older the author will discard his errors of taste." "As a matter of fact," said my friend, "the author's an alcoholic of over forty." "In that case," I answered, "I think the book is perfect rubbish." Does that seem to you unreasonable? There is a charm in the gay frolics of youth. But they do not become middle age. We can take with good humour the practical jokes that children love to play on us, but when they are indulged in by persons of mature age we can only regret that they should be so unfortunate as to suffer from arrested development. The medical profession describes persons thus afflicted as morons.

These remarks, which I warned you would be desultory, lead me, I hope without violence, to the second topic on which I told you I was going to talk to you. They lead me from the book to the author, and from reading to writing. Every writer who has attained a certain notoriety receives a great many letters from persons who wish to become authors and want to know how to do it. I am going to read to you now one such letter that I received a long time ago and the correspondence which ensued. The writer was a lady who lived in Boston, which as you know, its inhabitants look upon as the centre of American culture, and in Beacon Street, to live in which is an indication of wealth and consequently of social distinction.

My dear Mr. Maugham,

I trust that you will pardon a total stranger writing to you and will give a few minutes of your valuable time to answering a question which I am going to put to you. I am sure you are very busy and I would not take the liberty of asking your advice if I were not fully determined to take it. To cut a long story short my son is about to leave Harvard and has determined to adopt the profession of literature. His intention is to write chiefly fiction and I should be very grateful if you would tell me in a few words how he can best fit himself for such a career. I am anxious to do everything in my power to assist him.

>Cordially yours,
>FRANCES VAN BUREN HALE.

I was at the time staying in New York and I answered the letter promptly.

MY DEAR MRS. HALE,
Give your son a thousand dollars a year for five years and tell him to go to the devil.

>Yours very faithfully,
>W. S. MAUGHAM.

A thousand dollars then was of course worth a great deal more than it is now.

The lady replied by return of post.

MY DEAR MR. MAUGHAM,
I am entirely at a loss to understand your answer to my letter. I do not think my request was unreasonable and I cannot think that it deserved a reply which if I hesitate to call uncivil you will not be surprised if I consider strangely flippant in an author of your standing in the literary world. I regret that I troubled you and beg to remain,

>Yours truly,
>FRANCES VAN BUREN HALE.

To this I returned the soft answer that turneth away wrath.

MY DEAR MRS. HALE,
I am much grieved that you were displeased with my letter. I had no wish to be impolite and I was very much in earnest; I was brief, which I thought you wished me to be, and I gave you advice which I knew to be direct and which I thought was sensible. Your

son is about to leave Harvard and therefore may be presumed to possess at least the rudiments of a liberal education. I can imagine no better grounding for anyone who desires to be a writer, and from the address from which you write I judge that he has been brought up in affluent circumstances. He will doubtless have spent most of his life among ladies and gentlemen. This is a class which from a literary standpoint rests now under a cloud, but it ventures still to exist and it is well for the writer to know its manners and customs. Your son, I suppose, has led a sheltered life and at his age can hardly have gained much knowledge of the world. I do not know how better you can help him to acquire this than by taking the advice I gave you. On a thousand dollars a year he cannot starve, but if he is of an adventurous disposition (and unless he is he will not desire to be a writer) he will often find himself penniless and so obliged to do whatever he can to earn his dinner. That is not bad training. On this sum, moreover, he can travel all over the world, but only in conditions that will throw him in contact with all kinds and conditions of men. He will not be able to afford the luxury of respectability.

Besides, in telling him to go to the devil you will have explained to him that you mean him to attach the widest possible meaning to that hackneyed phrase. If he has any spirit he will soon find an infinite number of ways and means to carry out your suggestion and in five years he will have gathered experience and an acquaintance with men and women which cannot fail to be of great value to him as a writer. If at the end of this period he cannot write then you must console yourself with the reflection that he lacks what no thought of yours nor advice of mine can give him: Talent.

                Yours very faithfully,
                      W. S. MAUGHAM.

I did not receive an answer to this for nearly a week.

Dear Mr. Maugham,

I am sorry if I sounded a little abrupt, but I will frankly confess that I could make neither head nor tail of your first letter. Of course I see now that you had no wish to be discourteous or flippant. But all the same I don't think I quite agree with the things you say. Surely it is not necessary for an author to live in a disreputable way any more than it is necessary for a violinist or a poet to wear long hair. Miss Austen wrote her admirable novels without leaving the respectable circle in which she was born, and Mr. Henry James, whose novels I am sure you appreciate as highly as I do, never to my knowledge moved in any world but that to which he was entitled by his birth and position. It was my privilege to know Mrs. Wharton for many years and though she lived so long in France I can vouch from personal knowledge for the fact that she never ceased to be a refined and accomplished gentlewoman. I cannot help thinking this proves that there is no reason why an author should not write successful books without taking such a hazardous course as you propose for my son.

But I daresay I did not put my original question quite clearly. What I really wanted your advice about was more the technique of novel writing if you understand what I mean. That is a matter on which a young author naturally stands in need of guidance and I can only say on my behalf as well as on my son's that I should be sincerely grateful for any hints you can give him.

Yours most cordially,
FRANCES VAN BUREN HALE.

I replied to this letter as best I could, and at considerable length, but I will not read to you what I wrote, since I am going to tell you later much of what I said then. I received an answer after some days.

DEAR MR. MAUGHAM,

It is very good of you to have written me such a long and careful letter, but since I wrote to you last my son, after mature consideration, has decided to go into the bond business, which with his heritage and connections is of course very much more suitable.

I do not suppose you will leave this country without coming to Boston, and when you do Mr. Hale and I will have much pleasure in making your acquaintance. I shall be At Home on the first and third Wednesdays of the month until Lent.

Yours most cordially,
FRANCES VAN BUREN HALE.

I will admit that I hoped this correspondence would amuse you, but I did not read it only to make you laugh. I read it because it draws attention to what I think is the most important part of the writer's equipment. That is his personality. It may be a pleasant one or an unpleasant one. That doesn't matter. When you come down to brass tacks, the value of a work of art depends on the artist's personality. It is that which flavours his work with the peculiar tang that gives it interest. Now, I think it is in an author's power to mould his personality. Of course life will to some extent mould it for him, as it does for all of us: we are all creatures of circumstance and we should none of us be what we are but for our environment, and the happy accidents, chance encounters, trials, pains and pleasures which have befallen us. But his personality is the writer's stock-in-trade and it is worth his while by deliberate effort to develop it. All experience, even the most ordinary and insignificant, is grist to his mill. He should not sit around and wait for experience to come to him; he should go in search of it. He should expose himself willingly to all the vicissitudes of life, accepting pain as well as pleasure, failure as well as success, in the assurance that everything that happens to him will enrich him. Life is the novelist's business, and he can only know about it and write about it with truth and significance if he participates in it. But that is not enough. Without a great deal more than a nodding acquaintance with art and literature, his personality will remain incomplete. He should in short be a man of wide culture. So may he develop his talent and gain the power to infuse whatever he writes with the idiosyncrasy which is originality.

As you see I am asking a great deal, but even yet I haven't finished. It is no use for the writer to have a full, rich and cultivated personality unless he has also acquired the technique of the art of writing. Like every other author I receive a large number of manuscripts from persons unknown to me, and sometimes I read them. What surprises me is not so much the ineptitude of the stories the writers have to tell and the unskilfulness with which they tell them, but how execrably they are written. A person who wants to be a painter goes to an art school, a person who wants to be a pianist takes lessons, but it is only too plain that it never occurs to a person who wants to be a writer that he has anything to learn. Why should he think it is any easier to write than to play the piano or to paint? It isn't.

Our language is not an easy one to write and our grammar is monstrously difficult. None of us can expect never to make mistakes. The best we can hope is that we shall not make many. Unless things have changed very much since I was at school I cannot but think that English is very badly taught, with the lamentable result that few people are able to express themselves on paper briefly, plainly and correctly. One reason why in general the French write so much better than we do is that they are taught to write and we are not. Those of you who have read Mrs. Gaskell's *Life of Charlotte Brontë* will remember with what careful severity M. Héger corrected her grammar, her choice of words and her style. In the examination for the *baccalaureat* French composition is of paramount importance and it is to that part of their ordeal that students look forward with most apprehension.

It is not only the grammar that makes English a difficult language to write. English has an enormous vocabulary—how large you can see for yourselves by comparing a French dictionary of synonyms with Roget's *Thesaurus*. The French dictionary is a slim volume of three hundred loosely printed pages; Roget is a volume of nearly a thousand pages printed in double columns. English, as everybody knows, is an amalgam of several languages, and it is this amalgam that has made it the rich and poetic language it is and so enabled our race to produce the greatest body of great poetry that the modern world has seen. But it may be that it is just this richness that has made it more difficult for us to write prose. We have found it hard to write with the clarity, precision and simplicity of the French.

There are doubtless several ways of writing English prose, but I suppose the two principal ones are the plain and coloured or the simple and flowery. The outstanding example in our literature of the plain is Swift and of the flowery Jeremy Taylor.

I don't suppose you want me to go into the history of English prose, even if I were competent to do so, and I will only say that until the sixteenth century it was on the whole simple and straightforward. If you could bring yourselves to read one of Caxton's later prefaces you would see how true that is. It is as good prose as ever has been written in English. Then, for a variety of reasons, among others the introduction to the reading public of the great Tudor translations, the language became highly coloured, elaborate, often very fine and poetic. A great many new words were introduced and as the ordinary reader didn't know what they meant the familiar word was added and so what is known as the doubleton came into favour. It resulted in making English writing more verbose and unwieldy than it need have been. The doubleton will be familiar to those of you who go to church in the phrase of the Prayer Book: when we assemble and meet together. The word 'assemble' was new to the illiterate person and so the words 'meet together' were added to tell him what it meant. But the doubleton has served its purpose and when a modern author, whose name I shall not tell you, writes of the rich and opulent appearance of one of his characters I think he is ill-advised.

It was not till Dryden, who had gone to school with the French writers of his day, that an attempt was made to make English prose supple and simple. This style of writing was brought to perfection by the writers of the reign of Queen Anne. We may admire the profuse beauty of Jeremy Taylor, the grandiloquence of Dr. Johnson and the sumptuous periods of Edmund Burke, but I think most of us find that a little of it goes a long way. For my part I prefer plain writing and I think it is more in the spirit of our day. But to write plainly is not a gift of nature: it has to be learnt. Of course one must write in the manner of one's own period. To try to write like the masters of the early eighteenth century would be absurd, but all the same to study them carefully cannot fail to help the modern writer to write well, clearly, simply and precisely.

I ask myself sadly from time to time why these people whose manuscripts I read want to adopt the profession of literature when it is only too plain that they lack even the elements of the necessary equipment. Sometimes obviously it is because they think it is an easy way to make money. They are grossly mistaken. A plumber or an electrician can make a better and a steadier income than all but very few authors and he enjoys moreover the respect of the community, which an author can seldom hope to do.

Sometimes they want to adopt this hazardous calling because they think the author's life is easy and pleasant. It is pleasant. He is not confined to an office. He can work where and when he likes; and the only tools he needs are paper and a pen or a typewriter. But it is an error to think the author's life is an easy one. It is a whole-time job. It needs industry, perseverance and infinite patience. However experienced you are, however competent, you never entirely conquer the difficulties of technique, and by the time you have learnt to write, not as well as you'd like to, none of us ever does that, but as well as you can, it is very likely that you will have nothing more to write about.

Others again wish to write because they seek fame. That is a natural and not ignoble ambition. But it is a will-o'-the-wisp. Of the many thousand writers who burden the earth very few achieve fame and of those who do there are fewer still whose fame outlasts their lifetime. A few years go by and works which seemed destined to immortality are discovered to be unreadable. In my twenties we all read George Meredith with passionate enthusiasm. I have not met for a long time a young man of literary inclinations who had read even one of his novels.

The only valid and sensible reason I know for adopting the profession of literature is that you have so strong and urgent a desire to write that you cannot resist it. Unfortunately, however, the strength and urgency of your desire do not guarantee that you will write anything that is worth writing. But of course if someone is under that compulsion to write, for a compulsion it should be, that doesn't matter. He may succeed or he may fail, but in any case he will have enjoyed the intense pleasure of creation and fulfilled himself. He will lead a life of inexhaustible interest and enjoy, as few can in this world of to-day, the inestimable pleasure of freedom.

Printed in Great Britain by Butler & Tanner Ltd., Frome and London. Published for the National Book League, 7 Albemarle Street, London, W.1, by the Cambridge University Press, Bentley House, Euston Road, London, N.W.1.